INTRODUCTION

Did you know 25% of Americans have so much clutter in their two-car garages they can't park one car in them?
And 32% only have room to park one car![i]

Then there are those of us who pay someone else to store our stuff - 10% of Americans spend $1,000 a year renting storage space.

Clutter is sneaky and has a way of taking over our lives - from that junk drawer (or two) in the kitchen to the closet full of clothes that you "might" wear some day to the "heirlooms" you're hanging onto in case the kids might want it someday.

Instead of hanging onto the clutter, why not get rid of it - and make some cash at the same time?

(And we're not talking about spending four hours on a Saturday morning, getting up before sunrise to sell your stuff in a garage sale. We're talking about a "virtual" sale that will bring in more money!)

Are you ready to get started?

CHAPTER 1: THE COST OF CLUTTER

Americans spent 2.5 days every year searching for lost items.[ii]

By the time we turn 60, we will have lost nearly 200,000 things. [iii]

The United States has between 45,000 and 60,000 storage facilities[iv]*.... that's about four times the number of Starbucks stores in the country.*[v]

One in 10 people spends $1,000 a year (or more) in personal storage.

I recently worked with a client who had moved in with her parents to help them after one parent had surgery. She had decluttered and purged a lot of things before she moved, but still had enough stuff to fill up a 10' x 20' storage unit. Originally, the plan was only to stay with her parents for a few months, but then COVID-19 hit, and she stuck around a little longer.

By the time we worked together, not only had her stuff been in storage for more than a year - she had paid to move it all - twice!

Inside that storage unit we found:

- Boxes of books she had already read and wasn't using for reference
- A set of Kitchenaid cookware, she purchased for $300, 5 years ago.
- A box of dishes she purchased from a thrift store for $20.
- A Hamilton Beach blender she purchased 10 years ago for $25

- Kitchen utensils purchased at the Dollar Tree
- A set of china passed down in her family that no one had ever used
- And much more.

Client's storage unit full of items the client hadn't seen in a year.

Consider the fact that she was spending $200 a month in storage fees, that's $2,400 a year.

Now I ask you: Is that old $300 set of cookware worth $2,400?
No it is not.

If she got rid of everything in storage, she could purchase a brand new set of Calaphon cookware for about $600.

See where we're going with this?

The result?

We downsized just about everything in her storage unit - selling some items and donating others. Not only did she get a sizable tax deduction for her donations, she made several thousand dollars selling what she wasn't using. Money she can put toward buying brand new stuff when she moves into her own house.

Chances are, in your closets, garage, guest room or storage unit you too have items that aren't getting used and could be sold online.

CHAPTER 2: SORT IT OUT

Before you figure out what to sell, you're going to need to sort through your items. You could start small, like a junk drawer or a closet. Or you can start somewhere that will make a big impact - like your bedroom or the kitchen (two of the most cluttered areas in the home).

What you'll need:

- Trash can/trash bags
- Shredder
- Zipper bags
- Zip ties
- Boxes/bags for sorting (at least three)
- Timer

When you sort through everything, you'll create a couple of piles:

- Keep
- Don't keep (donate)
- Sell

How To Determine What To Keep And What To Get Rid Of

I created a flow chart to ask yourself some questions about each item.

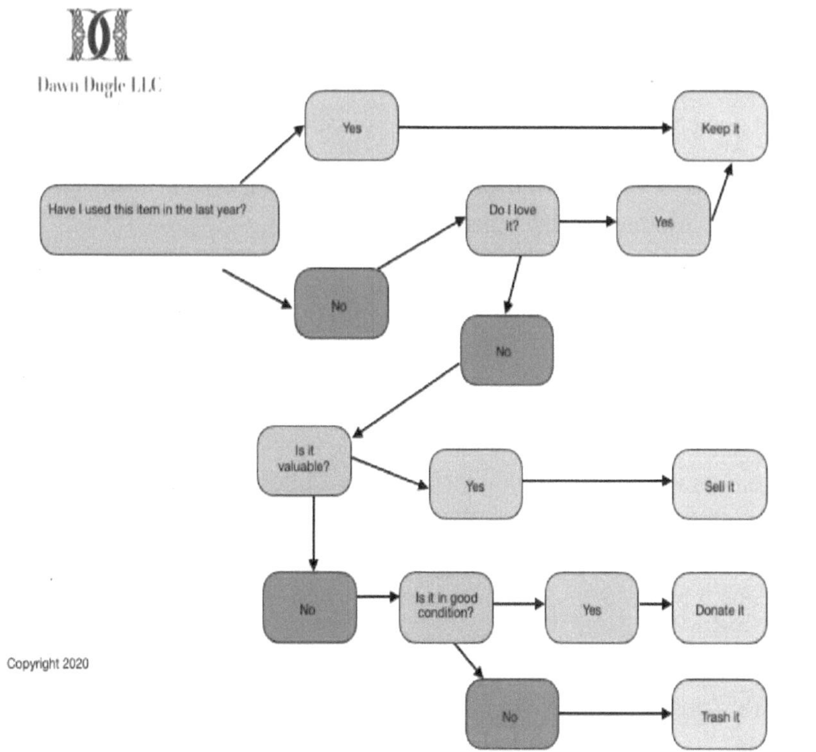

Have you used the item in a year?

> If yes - keep it.
> If no - ask yourself if you love it. If the answer to that question is yes, then keep it.

From there, it's a matter of where it goes.

Valuable items can be sold.

Items that aren't of value but still in good condition can be donated to your local charity.

Items that aren't in great condition (broken, stained, missing pieces) need to be thrown away.

I'll be the first to admit. I'm Scottish and that means I'm incredibly frugal about things. In the past, I've had stacks of "to be fixed" items that I intended to get around to fixing.. but guess what? I never did. And those things took up space.

If you don't have the parts or the time to fix something, throw it away.

By the way - if you can't remember the last time you used or wore something? Remember my mantra:

> *If I don't know, it's got to go.*

The "Skinny" Clothes

85% of women have clothes in their closet that don't fit. And nearly half of those women hang onto the clothes because it might fit them "some day".

I've done it too.

The problem with those "skinny clothes" (or their ugly twin the "fat clothes) is that if you ever get into those clothes again, they're likely going to be out of style.

In the meantime, they hang in the closet, mocking you. Making you feel bad about your life choices.

It's time to let them go. Let them have a new life where they can be worn and not have to give you a guilt trip every time you open the closet.

When you get back down to that size in the future, you can celebrate by buying new clothes that you love.

Guilt Items

My client with the huge storage unit? There was a lot of "guilt" furniture in there.

You know the kind I'm talking about - that furniture that was handed down to you in the family and it came with a load of guilt. The "should keep" stuff.

> *I should keep this because my aunt gave it to me and she's no longer with us.*

> *I should keep this because it was a Christmas present from my mom 10 years ago, and she might come for a visit.*

The problem with that guilt furniture and those "should keep items"? They're often not your style and have likely outlived their usefulness.

I toted around a 200-year-old loveseat that had been handed down through the family, going all the way back to Scotland. The doggone thing was so fragile, it would get broken during every interstate move (four of them) and then I'd have to get it fixed at an antique furniture repair shop. There are very few of those left.

Not to mention the fact that this loveseat was too fragile to sit upon. The only creature brave enough to sit on it was my cat. A very fragile, antique… cat seat.

I finally bit the bullet, and put it on consignment. Not only did I make $90 from the sale, but someone is giving it a nice new home. And I no longer have to worry that it will get broken during a move.

It was a weight off my shoulders.

If you are the *keeper* of furniture or items you wish to "hand down" to your children or grandchildren, keep this in mind:

> *The children likely don't want them.*

Generation X (those born between 1965 and 1980) and Millennials (1981-1996) aren't in the market for dark heavy furniture and full sets of china. And they don't want collections of Hummels and Lladro.[vi]

But every family is different.

I recommend talking to your adult children and grandchildren about your furniture and keepsakes. Talk to them about the important things you want them to keep - a family heirloom with a story.

One client of mine marked her “important” keepsakes with little written stories tucked away in the base of the collectibles or furniture where her daughters would find it when she passed away.

Another idea is to have a “Name it and Claim it” party during the holidays. Give each person a different colored sticky notepad and let them go through the house and mark what they would want, letting them know if it’s not claimed, you’re donating it or selling it after the first of the year.

My parents did that with my brother and me and also shared the stories behind the important things they wanted handed down in our family (which wasn’t much). It took a lot of the burden off of both sides, because now my parents don't have to hang onto items that are just getting in the way.

Bad Memories

A client called me up one day to help her declutter because: “I have a bunch of collectibles to sell,” she told me excitedly on the phone.

When we started going through her house to sort through everything, I noticed she had nearly a hundred Christmas decorations that were still in their original packaging. And in her guest closet, she had a series of stuffed bears from a clothing retailer. The retailer had released the bears in the late 90s.

“What’s the story behind all of these?” I asked.

She went on to tell me that she bought all of these items in the period right after her divorce. It was a “dark time” and she was glad she didn’t have to go through that again.

The more we talked about it, the more she realized the bad memories that were attached to these items. Instead of trying to sell them, and having to hang onto them a little longer, she decided to donate the entire lot to charity.

A few days after the donation, she told me she felt so much better and had no idea that stuff had been weighing her down for so long.

My storage unit client went through all of her pictures and keepsakes and realized a good chunk of them were from ex-boyfriends.

“What am I going to do when I meet my soulmate and have kids? Show them these old photos and say ‘here’s mommy with another man!’ It’s ridiculous now that I think about it,” she laughed.

She got rid of the pictures, donated most of the gifts - except for the gold jewelry. Those she took to a store that bought gold and made a pretty tidy sum for it.

Bottom line is: if you’re keeping something that doesn’t make you feel good, why are you keeping it?

Best practices:

- Going through a closet can take anywhere from four hours to an entire day, depending on the size of the closet.
- The kitchen could take a weekend.
- Break big tasks down into small increments of time. Use a timer to remind yourself to take breaks and hydrate!

CHAPTER 3: SELLING YOUR ITEMS

Prepare yourself.

When you get ready to sell your items, you're going to have an idea in your head of what it *should* sell for.
That number is likely close to what you paid for it.
But your number is likely *not* what someone else will pay for it now.

> *The "Endowment Effect" is where we give something that we already own a much higher value than if we were to go out and purchase it brand new.*[vii]

When you sell something online, you want to see what people are willing to pay for it.

Questions:

- What are you selling?
- What is it selling for online - in your area?
- What does it sell for brand new - right now?

That last question is very important.

In 2008, I purchased an LCD TV for $700. Twelve years later I went to sell it, along with a Roku box. Brand new, the same TV was selling for $200. My rule of thumb is to offer it for sale at 50% of that "new now" price - so $100. I couldn't even get someone to pay $50 for it, so I ended up donating it to charity.

> *Repeat after me: It doesn't matter what I paid for it. It only*

matters what people are willing to spend for it now.

Research your items on eBay, Etsy, local consignment stores, Facebook Marketplace and a straight up Google search.

Preparing The Item For The Online Listing

First step - clean it up. Dust it. Wipe off the fingerprints. Remove clutter from the tops of tables. You want this thing looking good in the photos.

Measure it. Get the dimensions. All sides. Height, width, depth, weight (if applicable).

Prepare the background. If you can get the item in front of a white or neutral background, it will look better in photos.

You want to "stage" the item for sale. If it's a table, show it with place settings. If it's a piano, show it ready to play. Show it in use.

Take photographs - wide shots and closeups. Open the doors and take pictures of it that way. Take some photos with a ruler or measuring tape right beside it, so people can see how tall it is in the photo.

Bad Example

This is a bad example because there's so much clutter on top of this table, it's hard to see if it would be of use in a buyer's home. Plus, it's dirty.

Good Example

This is a good example because the couch for sale is staged in front of a neutral background and showed "in use".

Write The Story

In early 2020, my parents were downsizing. They had a piano from my Great Aunt Hazel who had passed away years earlier. No one in the family wanted the piano and we were having a hard time finding a charity to take it.

I took a shot with Facebook Marketplace and wrote this:

> *This 1963 upright Gulbransen piano has only had one owner. My Great Aunt Hazel bought it brand new and took such good care of it throughout her lifetime.*
>
> *She taught every kid in our family how to play piano (including myself) and routinely entertained us with Christmas carols, church hymns and*

party favorites (mine was "The Entertainer" from "The Sting").

Two years ago, Aunt Hazel passed away at the age of 103 and no one has played it since. We're about to downsize and want to see this go to a good home where another family will love it as we have.

It's in PRISTINE condition.
Regularly tuned.
Walnut wood with a satin finish.
36" tall
56" long
(The piano bench comes with it.)

It needs a good home - so make us an offer and come get it.

This piano that no one wanted to come get for free, sold for $200. The woman who purchased it said it was the story that sold her on it.

There's something to be said for a story.
If you have a story for your item, tell it.

You'll also note in that example, I also included the relevant details - the year it was made, the color, the dimensions.

I also gave it a great headline: Gulbransen Upright Piano Needs a Good Home (MAKE OFFER)

Make sure you're clear on what you're seeing:
- Clear headline
- Entice with a story
- Give as many details as you can: type of wood, number of dishes, measurements
- Is it a smoke-free or pet-free home? Say that in the ad.
- Do you want people to "make offer" or is your price firm?
- Check your spelling and grammar

The piano I sold on Facebook Marketplace:

CHAPTER 4: FACEBOOK MARKETPLACE

It used to be Craigslist was the place to sell stuff you no longer wanted. Now, it's Facebook Marketplace. The great thing about Marketplace is it is tied to people's Facebook accounts, so you see their identifying information (their photo and their city), along with their rating on Marketplace.

I have a 5-star rating on Marketplace because buyers have rated me on our interactions. I've been rated as having "fair pricing" and "on-time meetup" among other things.

Badges

Based on your activity on Marketplace

Highly Rated

4-stars or higher rating from at least 4 buyers

Very Responsive

Typically replies to messages in under an hour

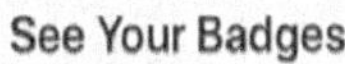

Seller Ratings

Those ratings can go the other way too. If a buyer attempts to scam you or simply doesn't show up on time, you can rate *them* in Marketplace. That means when someone is attempting to purchase what you're offering, you see their ratings and can make an informed decision about doing business with them.

Likewise, if you have a great interaction with your buyer, give them a good rating.

Getting Your Ad Online

Go into your Facebook news feed and look for the Marketplace icon (it looks like a little store).

On Mobile:

- Go to Marketplace
- Select "Sell"

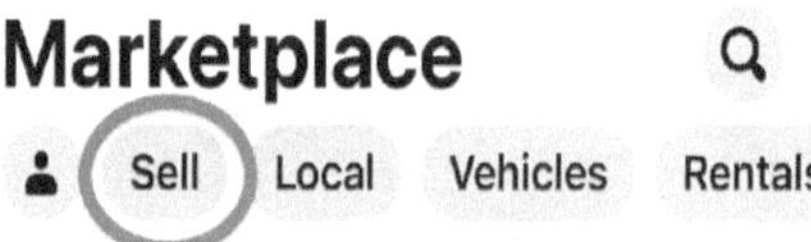

- Under Create New Listing, you'll likely choose "items"

Create New Listing

Homes for Sale or Rent

Jobs

On Desktop:

- Go to Marketplace
- Select "+Create New Listing"
- Then select "Item for Sale"

On both you'll then enter the details about the item:

- Add photos (up to 10)
- A title for your listing
- The price
- Category

- Condition
- Description (this is where you'll tell a story about it)
- Product tags

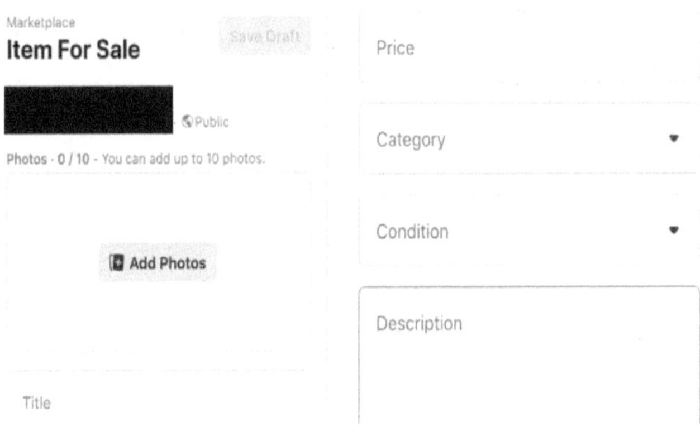

On the next screen you'll put in your location and delivery method - local pick up or shipping.

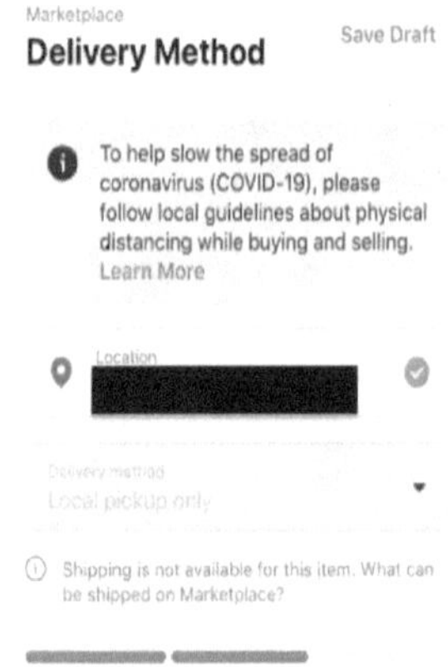

Then, if you are a member of any selling groups, you'll get the chance to post it in those groups, as well as on Marketplace itself.

List Publicly

Marketplace

Marketplace items are public and can be seen by anyone on or off Facebook.

List in Your Groups

You can list in up to 20 groups.

Finally - hit publish.

The Curb Alert

If you have big items that you just want to get rid of, Facebook Marketplace lets you post those as well. Those are the "curb alert" items.

Instead of giving it a price, the price is $0.

I would also put "Free" in the title of the posting.

This doesn't excuse you from taking good photos of the thing, or giving measurements, because people will inundate you with questions if not.

More Examples

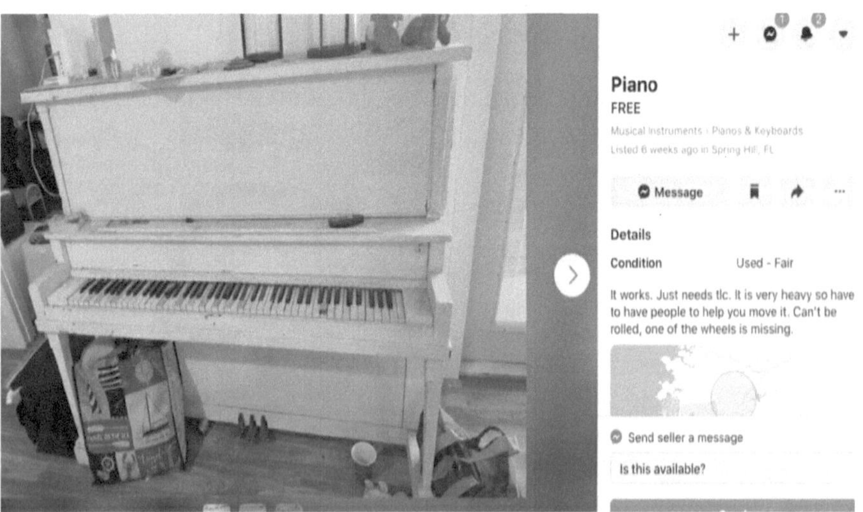

This person is trying to *give away a piano*, but the photo is terrible. It's not even clear what you're looking at.

On the left is the piano I sold for $200. On the right is that piano that the seller can't give away and has been on Facebook Marketplace for six weeks.

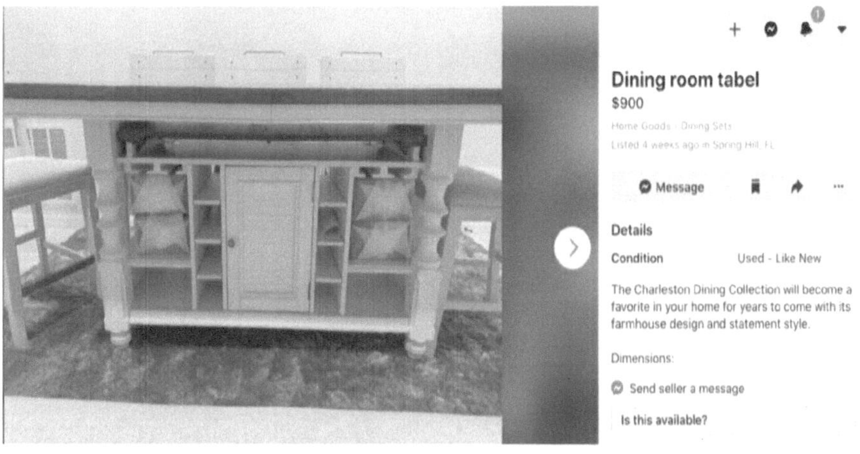

Spelling is important when you're putting an article up for sale. This "tabel" will not be found when someone is looking to buy a "table".

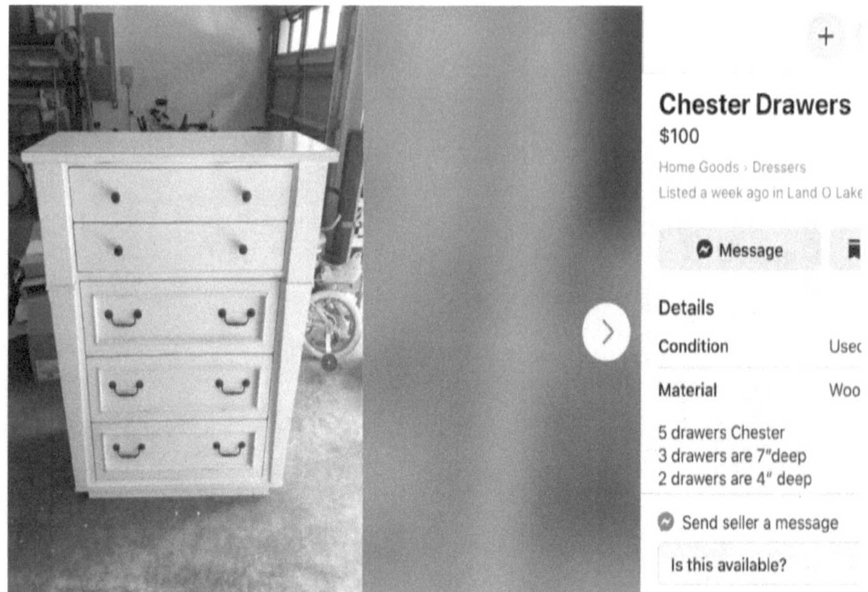

This item is not a "Chester Drawers" it's a *chest of drawers*, or a *dresser*.

Head Bordr

FREE

Again - they won't be able to give this away if it's not spelled correctly.

CHAPTER 5: SOLD!

When you post things on Facebook Marketplace for sale, potential buyers will contact you through the Messenger app.

They will have questions.

Sometimes those questions were answered in the ad.

It can be irritating when someone doesn't read the entire thing, but I look at it this way - they're so excited to have found something they're looking for - they couldn't wait another second to reach out to you about it!

So - be nice when they message you.

Be patient.

And be safe.

These are some of my personal "best practices" when it comes to meeting a buyer:

Can you meet the buyer somewhere public?

I like to meet someone in the parking lot of the local police or fire station. I will get there early, tell the people inside what I'm doing and then wait outside.

Sometimes I'll meet a buyer near the entrance of a grocery store. There are cameras there and a lot of people.

If the item isn't mobile, can you drag it into the garage or your covered porch? Especially in the time of COVID-19, you don't want strangers coming into your house.

Have someone with you when you meet the buyer.

If you’re arranging a time to meet, don’t tell the person you’re “going out” or “won’t be home” at a certain time. Just say *“that won’t work, how about xx instead?”*

Only accept cash.

It’s good to make sure you have that in your ad, and reiterate it in your communications with potential buyers.

After The Sale

First of all - don't ever list something as "sold" until it's actually sold. Facebook Marketplace will allow you to list something as "pending", but I don't do that very often unless it's a hot item that a lot of people are interested in.

After the sale, make sure you mark the item as sold. Facebook will ask you if you sold it to someone on Marketplace and who you sold it to. This is where you can also rate the buyer. Give them a good rating and some feedback to help their profile - if they've earned it.

BIBILOGRAPHY

[i] Becker, J. (2020, June 01). 21 Surprising Statistics That Reveal How Much Stuff We Actually Own. Retrieved from https://www.becomingminimalist.com/clutter-stats/

[ii] Pixie Technology Inc. (2018, June 26). Lost and Found: The Average American Spends 2.5 Days Each Year Looking For Lost Items Collectively Costing U.S. Households $2.7 Billion Annually in Replacement Costs. Retrieved November 18, 2020, from https://www.prnewswire.com/news-releases/lost-and-found-the-average-american-spends-25-days-each-year-looking-for-lost-items-collectively-costing-us-households-27-billion-annually-in-replacement-costs-300449305.html

[iii] Lost and Found. (2015, April 23). Retrieved November 18, 2020, from https://www.swnsdigital.com/2012/03/lost-and-found/

[iv] Curry, K., & Harris, A. (2020, May 29). U.S. Self-Storage Industry Statistic [UPDATED MARCH 2020]. Retrieved from https://www.sparefoot.com/self-storage/news/1432-self-storage-industry-statistics/

[v] Statista. (2020, September 15). Starbucks stores: U.S. and international. Retrieved from https://www.statista.com/statistics/218366/number-of-international-and-us-starbucks-stores/

[vi] Arvedlund, E. (2019, May 04). Millennials don't want heavy antiques, brown furniture; they crave 'Mad Men'-era stuff. Retrieved November 18, 2020, from https://www.post-gazette.com/business/money/2019/05/04/Millennials-don-t-want-heavy-antiques-brown-furniture-they-crave-Mad-Men-era-stuff/stories/201905040037

[vii] Bockarova, M. (2016, August 05). How Will the "Endowment Effect" Affect You? Retrieved November 18, 2020, from https://www.psychologytoday.com/us/blog/romantically-attached/201608/how-will-the-endowment-effect-affect-you

www.ingramcontent.com/pod-product-compliance
Lightning Source LLC
LaVergne TN
LVHW040939150826
845672LV00008B/2451
9798472094917